S0-CJQ-691

FLATBED TRUCKS

by Katie Chanez

Cody Koala
An Imprint of Pop!
popbooksonline.com

abdobooks.com
Published by Pop!, a division of ABDO, PO Box 398166, Minneapolis,
Minnesota 55439. Copyright © 2020 by POP, LLC. International copyrights
reserved in all countries. No part of this book may be reproduced in any
form without written permission from the publisher. Pop!™ is a trademark
and logo of POP, LLC.

Printed in the United States of America, North Mankato, Minnesota

052019
092019

THIS BOOK CONTAINS
RECYCLED MATERIALS

Cover Photo: Robert Carner/Alamy
Interior Photos: Robert Carner/Alamy, 1; iStockphoto, 5, 7 (top),
7 (bottom left), 7 (bottom right), 8, 11, 12, 15, 17, 18–19, 20, 21

Editor: Meg Gaertner
Series Designer: Sophie Geister-Jones

Library of Congress Control Number: 2018964596
Publisher's Cataloging-in-Publication Data
Names: Chanez, Katie, author.
Title: Flatbed trucks / by Katie Chanez.
Description: Minneapolis, Minnesota : Pop!, 2020 | Series: Construction
    vehicles | Includes online resources and index.
Identifiers: ISBN 9781532163333 (lib. bdg.) | ISBN 9781644940068 (pbk.) |
    ISBN 9781532164774 (ebook)
Subjects: LCSH: Trucks--Juvenile literature. | Construction equipment--
    Juvenile literature. | Construction industry--Equipment and supplies--
    Juvenile literature.
Classification: DDC 629.224--dc23

Hello! My name is

Cody Koala

Pop open this book and
you'll find QR codes like
this one, loaded with
information, so you can
learn even more!

Scan this code* and others like it while you read,

or visit the website below to make this book pop.

popbooksonline.com/flatbed-trucks

*Scanning QR codes requires a web-enabled smart device with a QR code reader app and a camera.

Table of Contents

The Flatbed Truck Can Help!

A construction worker needs very long pipes for a job. The pipes do not fit in other vehicles. Only a flatbed truck can carry them.

Watch a video here!

A Flatbed Truck's Job

Flatbed trucks **haul** objects.

They can carry many things.

Some carry steel beams or

wood for buildings. Others

haul very large objects, such

as houses.

Learn more here!

Flatbed trucks can even carry other vehicles. They might carry cars. They might carry bulldozers or other construction vehicles.

Trucks carrying large objects use a sign that says "oversize load." This warns other drivers on the road.

Chapter 3

Parts of a Flatbed Truck

Flatbed trucks have two key parts. The first part is the truck tractor. Truck tractors have powerful engines. The second part is the **trailer**. Truck tractors pull trailers.

Learn more here!

The trailer in a flatbed truck is long and flat. It has no sides or top. **Cargo** can be loaded onto the trailer from every side.

Flatbed trailers are not the only kind of trailer. Other trailers have sides and a top.

Workers use straps or chains to hold the cargo in place. This keeps the cargo from falling off the trailer.

Chapter 4

Types of Flatbed Trucks

Most flatbed **trailers** are **level**. But drop-deck trailers are higher in the front and lower in the back. These trailers can hold tall **cargo** and still fit under bridges.

Complete an activity here!

Lowboy trailers sit even closer to the ground. But they get higher in the back.

Wheels fit underneath the trailers. Lowboy trailers can carry the tallest cargo.

People use small flatbeds
for construction projects and
on farms. These flatbeds are
similar to pickup trucks.

But they don't have sides
on their **truck beds**. Big or
small, flatbed trucks are
useful tools.

Making Connections

Text-to-Self

Have you ever seen a flatbed truck? What cargo was it carrying?

Text-to-Text

Have you read a book about a different kind of truck? How is that truck similar to or different from a flatbed truck?

Text-to-World

Flatbed trucks can carry cargo. What are other ways to move cargo from one place to another?

Glossary

cargo – objects that are being moved.

haul – to move something, often over a long distance.

level – flat.

trailer – a vehicle that cannot move on its own, but instead is pulled behind another vehicle.

truck bed – the back of a truck where cargo can go.

Index

Online Resources

popbooksonline.com

Thanks for reading this Cody Koala book!

Scan this code* and others like it in this book, or visit the website below to make this book pop!

popbooksonline.com/flatbed-trucks

*Scanning QR codes requires a web-enabled smart device with a QR code reader app and a camera.